YOUR KNOWLEDGE HA

CW00498272

- We will publish your bachelor's and
  master's thesis, essays and papers

- Your own eBook and book -
  sold worldwide in all relevant shops

- Earn money with each sale

Upload your text at www.GRIN.com
and publish for free

Teleworking in Nigeria. Issues, Prospects and Challenges

Ademolu Adediran

GRIN

Bibliographic information published by the German National Library:

The German National Library lists this publication in the National Bibliography; detailed bibliographic data are available on the Internet at http://dnb.dnb.de.

ISBN: 9783346517883
This book is also available as an ebook.

© GRIN Publishing GmbH
Nymphenburger Straße 86
80636 München

All rights reserved

Print and binding: Books on Demand GmbH, Norderstedt, Germany
Printed on acid-free paper from responsible sources.

The present work has been carefully prepared. Nevertheless, authors and publishers do not incur liability for the correctness of information, notes, links and advice as well as any printing errors.

GRIN web shop: https://www.grin.com/document/1140058

TELEWORKING IN NIGERIA: ISSUES, PROSPECTS AND CHALLENGES

Ademolu Adediran

Master of Industrial and Personnel Relations Programme, Department of Sociology, University of Ibadan, Oyo State, Nigeria. June 2021.

ABSTRACT

Teleworking practices have been increasing internationally due to the global expansion of organizational boundaries it offers businesses. It had been perceived as a crucial response to competitive imperatives by top multinationals even prior to the Covid-19 pandemic.

In Nigeria however, it was the Covid-19 lockdowns that obligated the adoption of teleworking practices by organizations, as a means of business continuity. The benefits teleworking offered in the business environment during the period have since brought about conjectures it could become part of the "new normal' even after the pandemic. Despite this, the globally reported prospects and challenges for employees and organizations have largely not been investigated in the Nigerian context.

The paper, through critical review of secondary data aims to explore the perceived prospects, success factors, and challenges of this emerging work arrangement for Nigerian employees and organizations.

i

CHAPTER ONE

INTRODUCTION

Telework arrangements are becoming part of organizational structures internationally due to the increasing pressures on cost-saving, and in a bid to increase employee productivity. The improvement in quality and expansion of internet services and the merging of voice, data, and video over common frameworks have made teleworking a viable option, or perhaps a requirement, for medium to large-sized businesses in today's marketplace (Ingham, 2006; Richard Ye, 2012).

Also, in responding to competitive imperatives, a visible pointer of the changing work environment is the global expansion of organizational boundaries. In this regard, the creation of virtual organizations is the only response to the current chaos of global competition (Watson-Manheim *et al.*, 2002; Helms and Raiszadeh, 2002; Thorne, 2005).

Organizations are making greater use of teleworking teams as fundamental parts of their functioning. Multinational organizations like IBM, Boeing, AT&T, and Merrill Lynch are making a success of virtual telework arrangements in their global operations. Microsoft founder, Bill Gates, of recent claimed that by the year 2050, 50% of workers globally will be teleworkers. These factors and more have led to companies feeling even more challenged to initiate flexible arrangements for the new "corporate office." (Morgan, 2004; Jackson *et al.,* 2006; Kowalski and Swanson, 2005).

Asides from being a response to competitive imperative in global business, the COVID-19 pandemic and lockdowns also necessitated the adoption of teleworking by many organizations as a means of business continuity, and in a bid to stay safe. The lockdowns affected all sectors of the economy, necessitating quick adoption of telework arrangements due to the need to reduce social and physical contact of persons. The lockdowns influenced nations and individuals in different ways, from mental, to social and then financial dimensions, and a catastrophe of such enormity cannot leave without its marks. A major shift it has brought about is the adoption of teleworking and virtual meetings over the energy-intensive forms of transportation (Pan et al., 2020; McKeever, 2020; Petersen et al., 2020; Joseph et al., 2020).

The rise in teleworking during the pandemic has led to increased employee proficiency at using digital work tools, employers find it appeasing that work continues despite employees not being physically present in the office, organizations have employed diverse digital means to reach out to the needs of the consumers, while consumers have learned digital ways to have their needs met. Unlike physical meetings, online meetings are held when needed, and just like physical meetings they also require a lot of planning and strategy, with meeting time is strictly adhered to. These factors make the argument that teleworking helps in transforming organizations by enhancing employee efficiency and organizational performance tenable (Helms, 1996; Neufeld and Fang, 2005; Glenn and Dutcher, 2012; Alexander, 2020).

In Nigeria, despite the internationally perceived prospects, many firms and corporate organizations found teleworking an unacceptable work style before the outbreak of the coronavirus pandemic. Now many of these firms and corporate organizations have embraced the work-from-home style to remain in business.

Considering the possibility of a prolonged or recurring coronavirus outbreak and the need to maintain a competitive edge by expanding organizational boundaries while offering flexible work arrangements, it is not unlikely that there will continue to be an increase in teleworking, even after the pandemic. The aim of the paper is therefore to examine the prospects and challenges of telework and factors organizations need to consider when deploying a teleworking program in the Nigerian context based on a review of available literature and published global best practices.

CHAPTER TWO

TELEWORKING: MEANING, PRACTICES AND REQUIREMENTS

2.1. Meaning of Telework

The term "telework" was first developed by Jack Nilles in 1973. He used the terms to describe the working arrangement in which work is done in a location outside the traditional office space (JALA International, 2007). It is a working system in which employees do not have to commute or travel to a workplace such as an office building.

Teleworking involves a swap of the worksite, with interactions restricted due to the physical and psychological distance involved in the swap. In most cases the alternative worksite inferred by the definition above is home, telework centers and remote offices are however also alternatives (Feldman and Gainey, 1997; Hill *et al.,* 1998; Davis and Polonko, 2001; Baruch, 2001; Bailey and Kurland, 2002).

Whilst the telework concept dates back to the 70s, there is no generally accepted exact definition. This is also demonstrated by the many kinds of terms applied to it: telework, telecommuting, remote work, work-from-home, smart working, virtual work, e-work, etc. The 2002 European Framework Agreement on telework defined it as a form of organizing work using information and communications technology, in the circumstances of an employment relationship, where work which could be performed within the employer's premises, is constantly carried outside the premises. A teleworker is any ICT-using employee whose worksite at least on one occasion a month is outside of the employers according to The International Labor Office (ILO)" (Eurofound and the ILO, 2017).

2.2. Types and Practices

According to Huws *et al.,* 1997, the following are the various telework types and practices:

3

- Multi-site Teleworking: In this form, there is a rotation between working on the employer's premises and elsewhere. Usually, the alternative worksite is the home, it could also be a tele-cottage, telecentre, or some other outpost
- Tele-homeworking: refers to arrangements where work is based only in the employee home and executed for a single employer, with or without formal employee status. This type of teleworking generally involves fairly low-skilled work carried out by people who are tied to the home by the need to care for children or other dependents
- Freelance teleworking: Freelance teleworkers, in contrast to tele-homeworkers, work for different clients, rather than a single employer
- Mobile teleworking: Refers to professional, technical, and managerial work that can be carried out 'on the road'. Examples include traveling sales representatives, inspectors, or maintenance engineers. The new technologies, especially the development of portable equipment such as the notebook computer, the mobile telephone, the portable fax machine, have created the type of mobility that allowed an increase in this kind of arrangements
- Relocated back-office: The first four categories of teleworking involve activities which employees can carry out in isolation away from the employer's premises. Relocated back-office takes place on remote office sites. Many big companies have been noticed a rapid growth in specialist centers carrying out activities such as data entry, customer service, airline bookings, telephone banking, and mail-order. Challenges such as lack of promotion prospects, health and safety problems, and equal opportunities issues, for instance fairly low-paid work carried out by women are associated with these type of teleworking arrangement (HuwsU. *et al.,* 1997).

Conner (2003) notes three degrees of 'virtualness' to telework:

1) The teleworking or telecommuting arrangement where technology allows employees to work away from the office and each other
2) The front-line arrangement where front office activities are taken closer to the customer
3) The cyber link arrangement where many different organizations work together through technology to achieve set goals

2.3. Telework requirements

2.3.1. Organizational factors

Establishing a thriving teleworking program requires much more than simply providing good internet service and digital tools. Organizations have to begin by analyzing the primary issues and factors that must be handled appropriately. Some keys factors necessary for consideration include:

- Eligibility (of workers) – Selection criteria and requirements for participation
- Technological equipment
- Teleworker training and help desk support
- Remote worker management and performance evaluations
- Teleworking rules and policies
- Teleworking agreement and contract (Richard Ye, 2012; Ajayi, 2020).

2.3.2. Employee/Personal factors

The ideal telework candidate is one that demonstrates high level of professionalism, and is dependable, resourceful, and self-reliant. A good teleworking candidate should be a team player, good communicator, and knowledgeable on teleworking technologies (Richard Ye, 2012).

Working from home requires personal control over working hours, organization of the home space as well as negotiations among family members over the distribution of time and space (Felstead *et al.*, 2005). Ojala *et al.* (2014) highlights that while work-life balance is seen as a major benefit of teleworking, research finding as to whether work from home strengthens or weakens work/family harmony is contradictory.

Grant *et al.* (2013) found job effectiveness, well-being, and work/life balance to be key factors when exploring the impact of remote technology on individuals and groups. These three areas overlap and are interrelated to some extent, in that job effectiveness can be impacted negatively and positively by both well-being and work/life conflict.

Carrying out paid work from home offers not just the possibility of work-life balance but there are questions of identity which are central to understanding the mutually, fundamental connections between domestic and professional aspects of life (Tietze and Musson, 2010). Hence, there is a need for people to come to an understanding of teleworking from the perspective of their overall lives, with regard to the home, which influences every facet of our lives, especially health and well-being.

When work and home activities take place in the same physical space, boundaries between work and home can become obscure. Research findings back up claims that teleworkers work longer hours. While employees vary in how they handle work and activities outside work separate or overlapping, those who favor the integration of work into home activities are more likely to experience weaker boundaries. (Harker, Martin, and MacDonnell, 2012; Clark, 2000)

Kreiner *et al.* (2009) propose four approaches to managing the boundary between work and home which are: physical, behavioral, communicative, and home-based tactics. The absence of the usual physical and time-based boundaries of the office space is the challenge telework poses to boundary management.

The physical tactics involve employees involve creating separate space for work activities and switching off. For the time-based tactics, strategies such as walking the dogs at a fixed closing time, picking up children from school can be of help. Behavioral tactics relate mainly to digital technology such as turning devices off after work hours, shutting down the computer system, thereby eliminating chances of checking messages. An example of communicative tactics is getting family members to knock before entering the workspace. According to Kreiner (2006), boundary management is a question of individual preferences, but the ability to manage preference can reduce work-life conflict and increase job satisfaction levels.

Gorham (2006) calls for women to exercise management skills in the home such as delegation of responsibilities, efficient use of time and resources, and coordination of activities.

CHAPTER THREE

PROSPECTS AND CHALLENGES OF TELEWORK

As with any business decision, ideally, before choosing a teleworking arrangement, the prospects and benefits sought for all stakeholders need to be clearly understood.

The description of businesses that engage in teleworking as revolutionary and not limited by the physical organizational structures needs to be modulated by considering the prospects and challenges posed by teleworking arrangements (Baruch and Yuen, 2000; Watad and Will, 2003; Morgan, 2004; Thorne, 2005).

3.1. Prospects

3.1.1. Prospects for organizations

As teleworking proficiency is rising, employees are becoming more proficient at using digital work tools, this has enabled organizations to employ diverse means in reaching the needs of consumers while consumers have learned digital ways to have their needs met. Other documented possibilities for organizations include:

- Increased productivity as a result of work autonomy given to teleworking professionals. Work autonomy often serves as a motivator, leading to a willingness on the part of employee to work harder
- Cost-saving associated with office space and infrastructure, energy saved by working from home, the costs and safety impacts delivered through reduced travel requirements and congestions
- Teleworkers often remain at organizations for longer periods, positively affecting employee retention and reducing hiring costs. Wilsker (2008) found that 64% of employees would rather continue teleworking that earn a 20% pay rise. Such non-wage benefits also improve employees' morale, job satisfaction, and work-life balance

- Organizations can get to include people who were previously excluded from the talent pool due to parental responsibilities, physical disabilities, or being unable to travel the required distance from home to office. This is a critical benefit in times of global scarcity of talented human capital
- Reduction in sick leave as another financial benefit of teleworking arrangements to organizations (Kepczyk, 1999; Mann *et al.,* 2000; Ilozor and Ilozor, 2002; Patrickson, 2002; Heneman and Greenberger, 2002; Johnson, 2004; Kowalski and Swanson, 2005; Hamilton 2006; Meadows, 2007; Wilsker, 2008; Martinez-Sanchez 2008; Radcliffe, 2010; Dutcher 2012; Timbal and Mustabsat, 2016; Soenanto *et al.,* 2016; Alexander, 2020).

3.1.2. Prospects for employees

Teleworkers have the flexibility to shape their work environment motivates them to perform to the best of their ability. This reduces stress levels, improves well-being, work-life balance, and creativity. Other prospects for employees include:

- Reduced traveling time, exposure to traffic congestion, and the air pollution associated with it while conserving car fuel and transportation expenses
- Less pressure on the job and a better social life, work-life balance, and improved ability to think clearly and analyze issues logically
- Increased employee proficiency with digital work tools
- Increased job satisfaction because of a reduction in stress levels
- Affords dual-career couples a balance between work and home life
- Greater well-being especially in women as a result of being present in both work and family lives. A study by Kossek *et al.* (2006) found that greater autonomy associated with teleworking led to the less frequent occurrence of depression in women (Ahmadi *et al.,* 2000; Siha and Monroe, 2006; Kossek *et al.,* 2006; Swink, 2008; Grant *et al.,* 2013; Glenn-Dutcher, 2016; Richter *et al.,* 2020)

3.1.3. Benefits to the society

Teleworking can be of significant benefit to society in the areas of reduced air pollution, traffic congestion, and energy consumption. Traveling to work not only contributes to traffic congestion, air pollution, greenhouse gas emission, and lower levels of physical activity but it is also linked to overweight and obesity in the general population

- Increasing traffic congestion may be a motivating factor for embarking on teleworking arrangements. This factor is pertinent within the Nigerian context with the annual increase of 107.3% in vehicles and an average of 12 people dying daily due to road traffic accidents in the year 2019.
- Siha and Monroe (2006) posits that telework arrangements be used in the future as a carbon reduction technique
- Teleworking provides society with a wide range of options offered by electronic communication technology and the internet
- The Covid-19 experience has also taught us that teleworking can be a security practice in the event of pandemics. It can be used in such situations to ensure safety and provide for continuity of economic activity

(Bailey and Kurland, 2002; Siha and Monroe, 2006; Wen *et al.,* 2010; Soenanto *et al.,* 2016; Ajayi, 2020; Belzunegui-Eraso and Erro-Garces, 2020; Morikawa, 2020).

3.2. Challenges

3.2.1. Challenges for organizations

In seeming contrast to the growing awareness of teleworking arrangements internationally, the actual adoption is still a passive strategy within the business world in the Nigerian context and is hardly taken earnestly to be implemented as part of corporate-wide strategies.

The reasons for the lack of implementation include the perception that teamwork suffers, the potential negative impact on employees who have less time to socialize with co-workers, organizational information security worries, and the lack of global reach of broadband technologies. To these perceived constraints, flexible working arrangements are not always viewed as a priority in business.

Other challenges to organizations considering the establishment of teleworking arrangements are:

- Insurance of the home office environment and equipment: Legal issues surrounding virtual working arrangements and insurance, compensation, and other issues have not yet been established
- Security requirements relating to equipment and data movement: Abuse of information technology and communication tools, such as granting family members access to such resources, is a potentials pitfall of teleworking if employees are not properly managed throughout the process
- Unavailability and/or inadequacy of local laws governing activities at private residences
- Difficulty in the provision of remote technical support
- Supervision and tracking of productivity made tougher: Manager-subordinate trust can be negatively affected by teleworking due to the little face-to-face interaction and less feedback from managers. The monitoring cost of the manager is also higher and less efficient, as coordination would be more difficult (Kepczyk, 1999; Tidd, 1999; Johnson, 2004; Kowalski and Swanson, 2005; O'Brien and Hayden, 2007; Martinez-Sanchez *et al.,* 2008; Benjamin-Dada, 2020; Myjobmag, 2021)

3.2.2. Challenges for employees

In Nigeria, the rise in the adoption of teleworking came mostly as a measure by organizations to curb the spread of the Covid-19 virus. The crisis mode of the lockdown turned on in most organizations made teleworking seem rather stressful than usual. The situation gave workers little or no room to familiarize themselves with the digital work experience. Hence teleworking has affected even more people in unexpected ways. The common challenges facing teleworking in Nigeria are problems of erratic electricity, poor service by the internet service providers, and the perception that those who work flexible hours are not working. The belief that it is difficult to manage staff who work flexible hours also exists. Some teleworkers have claimed they are seen not only as doing less but also as being into cybercrime by some members of society.

For the individual worker, the following challenges of teleworking demand considerable management attention:

- Separation of work from home: Workers in teleworking arrangements often have difficulty in separating work from private life. This not only affects the teleworker, but also other residents and family relations as the teleworkers along with their partner and children in the home are often unprepared for such integration of paid work into the household. Despite work-life balance being one of the most cited benefits of teleworking, having to address family responsibilities during work hours increases stress among teleworkers. There is contradictory research as to whether teleworking improves or declines work/family harmony

- Isolation: workers in telecommuting arrangements not having immediate colleagues against whom they can compare their productivity hampers benchmarking and can result in weaker performance caused by a lack of positive peer pressure. It can lead to an increased feeling of alienation from the company's major decisions, as one of the peoples basic needs is to belong to specific groups

- Reduced career progression: Teleworking employees may enjoy fewer promotions in the work environment as a result of a lack of opportunities to engage in networking activities

- Loss of on-the-job training activities caused by a shrinkage in the core workforce, bringing with it a reduction in the value of human capital

- Longer working hours: inability to stick to a daily routine is not uncommon with teleworkers as 24/7 access to technology leads to work intensification and longer hours, with little respite from work

- Social dumping resulting from the export of jobs across national boundaries

- Physical and psychosocial health implication: Performing telework often requires continuous use of information technology and communication tools as well as visual display units. These can be associated with physical and psychosocial health problems.

Physical problems such as an increase in the risk of musculoskeletal disorders are likely especially for work carried out on non-ergonomic workstations. Associated sedentarism can contribute to the burden of chronic diseases like diabetes, cardiovascular diseases, obesity, and hypertension.

Psychosocial problems linked to the experience of telework are sleeping disorders, work-related stress, and social isolation (Ahmadi *et al.,* 2000; Mann *et al.,* 2000; Mirchandani, 2000; Lim and Teo, 2000; Nakazawa *et al.,* 2002; Conner, 2003; Mann and Holdsworth, 2003; Morahan-Martin and Schumacher, 2003; Sullivan, 2003; Hughes and Love, 2004; Tietze and Musson, 2003; Horwitz *et al.,* 2006; Moustafa-Leonard, 2007; Thomée *et al.,* 2007; Hoe *et al.,* 2012; Baytcom, 2013; Grant *et al.,* 2013; Nytimescion, 2013; González *et al.,* 2017; Alexander, 2020; Fosslien and West Duffy, 2020).

3.3. Role of HR/Management

Since offering employees flexibility increases motivation and reduces turnover, thus increasing profitability, it is essential for Human Resources Managers to contribute.

Areas, where HR can contribute to the success of teleworking arrangements include:

3.3.1. Communications

It is of importance that effective communication exists along with trust between employers and employees, particularly with little face-to-face time and with social relationships under pressure. Interpersonal communication is beyond things that are said. The facial expressions, tone, the body language of the speaker, and mode of delivery also play an important role. The absence of such features when communicating virtually can have a key influence on the conveyed message. A careful balance between online and physical meetings will have to be maintained to retain the interpersonal balance between virtual employees and management (Mann *et al.,* 2000; Siha and Monroe, 2006; IoD Policy Report, 2019; ILO, 2020a).

3.3.2. Performance Management

Maintenance of team performance and fulfillment of stakeholder commitments is a common challenge for manager in teleworking arrangements. Dialogues and collaboration between management and employee is key to effective teleworking (ILO, 2020b). The management of teleworkers requires a switch in management approach from measuring 'process' to measuring 'output'. Managers who display the need to control people are not likely to perform well as managers of teleworkers. Giving up control over employees and offering them more freedom, however, should not detract from the manager's role as leader and evaluator of performances. (Kurland and Egan, 1999; Allert, 2001; Stanford, 2003; Morgan, 2004; Horwitz *et al.,* 2006; Siha and Monroe, 2006; Curseu *et al.,* 2008; Sorensen, 2016 ILO, 2020a; ILO, 2020b).

3.3.3. Occupational Safety and Health (OSH)

The sudden switch involving a large number of organizations from traditional work arrangements to telework happened without much considerations for occupational safety and health, which would otherwise apply if working within employer's premises where there usually are clear roles and responsibilities regarding ensuring physical and mental wellbeing of employees (ILO, 2020c).

Psychosocial risks and ergonomics are commonly recognized challenges. Teleworking for extended periods under tough external situations can provoke higher levels of anxiety in workers. Employers, HR, supervisors, and OSH professionals need to be aware of the associated risks of full-time teleworking, and the resulting requirement to neutralize or eliminate them.

It is also important to update existing OSH policy documents and identify information and skills gaps, and put in place training, information provision, and communication actions to ensure that everyone has access to information about their rights and responsibilities in terms of organizational health and safety of the workforce in the given situation (Eurofound, 2020; ILO, 2020a; ILO, 2020d).

3.3.4. Legal and contractual implications

It is very important to spell out the conditions of teleworking arrangements as regards location, the reimbursement of teleworking-related costs, contractual changes, and notification methods in the event of barriers to carrying out work, illnesses, or work-related incidents. Organizations need to establish various legal angles to telework and have sufficient insurance policies in case a work-related accident occurs during teleworking.

Clarification of terms and conditions of employment while teleworking is also key. Insurance and legal implications regarding equipment and software used while teleworking might need to be reviewed and adjusted (ILO 2020a; Garg and Rijst, 2015).

3.3.5. Tailor working arrangements to the employee

Managers should take into consideration the employee's needs at the time, their working habits and abilities, and remember that it is not necessarily a suitable working practice for everyone. It is important to ensure that employees have the rights skills for effective teleworking. Employersare more likely to get it right when it comes to remote working practices if their approach is balanced and evaluated on a case-by-case basis (IoD Policy Report, 2019; Eurasia Review, 2020).

3.3.6. Training and development of teleworkers

The emerging telework situation will require both workers and managers to reassess old working habits and learn new skills and organizations will have to acknowledge that. This is pertinent to managing the situation effectively, safeguard employee wellbeing, and maintain the agreed performance metrics. Technological support and the provision of necessary tools along with appropriate training are key to successfulimplementation (IoD Policy Report, 2019; ILO 2020a).

3.3.7. Work-life balance

By keeping the workload feasible and setting unclouded, reasonable expectations as to the particular results to be achieved, employees are more enabled to sort out their time and tasks, in order to effectively balance their work commitments with personal lives and family duties (Porter and Kakabadse, 2006; Harker Martin and MacDonnell, 2012; Pathak *et al.,* 2015; Cartmill, 2020; ILO, 2020a).

3.3.8. Trust and Organizational culture

Employers that maintained prompt, clear and open communications with their workers and supporting employees about processes and potential risks associated with telework, and supported them through the process, have made the most from telework arrangements. Trust is an important element that binds all the aspects of teleworking together. Involved stakeholders such as the managers, teleworkers, and their colleagues will have to trust each other. Telework cannot be effective without trust (ILO, 2020d). Trust can be pro-actively built by organizations, even if teams are working remotely. Empowering workers to make decisions without fearing negative repercussions is a means of achieving this. If workers feel trusted, they will take initiative in solving problems and making decisions, which will translate to time effectiveness for the team. Ensuring that teleworkers are a fundamental part of the organization by transmitting the larger organizational culture to teleworkers, including the transmission of established norms and values that form common ground between the body of employees and the virtual worker is of essence (Morgan, 2004; Horwitz *et al.,* 2006; Curseu *et al.,* 2008; ILO, 2020e)

3.3.9. Change management

Implementing teleworking arrangements involves many changes in the organization, for example, how it operates, how it communicates and how employees function. These changes need to be understood and planned prior to the introduction of this organizational initiative to ensure that the resistance to change does not prevent the successful implementation of the teleworking arrangement. (Smith, 2005; Diefenbach, 2007; Meyer *et al.,* 2007)

3.3.10. Involvement of social partners in the design and implementation

Consulting worker/trade union representatives, informing their members of the benefits of teleworking and offering assistance in transitioning to working remotely, and using their extensive networks to share experiences, empower each other, and spread important information regarding working from home have a role to play in holding employers accountable regarding the safety of the workplace. Trade unions maintenance of active communication with the workers could also be beneficial (ILO, 2020a).

15

CHAPTER FOUR

CONCLUSION AND RECOMMENDATIONS

Teleworking, even though quite flexible for employees, poses both prospects and challenges. In Nigeria, the "crisis mode" the lockdown turned on in most organizations made teleworking appear rather stressful than usual. The situation gave workers little or no room to familiarize themselves with the digital work experience.

Challenges such as misconceptions that teleworkers do less or are into cybercrime, power supply and access to effective internet, feelings of alienation from major discussion and promotions, and difficulty separating work from private life confront workers in the Nigerian setting. For organizations, challenges include collaboration inefficiencies due to lack of proximity to other workers, organization information security concerns, remote technical support, and legal issues.

Despite these shortcomings, teleworking allows employees to connect in new ways, work more flexibly, and establish new patterns of work autonomy and leadership. Teleworking offers prospects such as enhanced digital skills of the workforce, improved job satisfaction levels, increased family time and work-life balance, reduced commuting time. Organizations benefit from increased productivity and increased morale/job satisfaction arising from work flexibility, greater organizational loyalty, decreased infrastructural expenses, increased staff retention, and reduction in hiring costs. Organizations that take part in green initiatives to reduce their impact on the environment could also integrate teleworking into the strategy to achieve the objectives of this initiative

Teleworking could become part of the "new normal' after the pandemic. The competitive edge it offers organizations through work flexibility which in turn increases motivation and reduces turnover, thus increasing profitability among other benefits cannot be overlooked. Hence organizations need to have practical and actionable measures for effective teleworking.

Within this parameter, the following recommendations are made to Nigerian organizations:

- Organizations should update policy documents and identify information and skills gaps, and put in place training and information provision to close the gaps

- Managers of teleworkers will need to adjust their management styles and performance measurement processes to include the changes in working conditions of personnel whilst ensuring that performance management all the same forms an integral part of the manager-employee relationship

- Involvement of social partners especially trade union representatives, informing them of the benefits of teleworking and offering assistance in transitioning to teleworking. Their extensive networks could help spread information and hold employers accountable regarding the safety of the workplace.

Teleworking is increasingly becoming part of organizations internationally because of the obvious benefits offered by these arrangements in the current business environment. Nigerian organizations have not capitalized on this new trend. The paper aimed to explore prospects of this work practice, challenges, and issues that may need to be addressed if this work practice is to be introduced.

If the predictions around the future projection of the number of international teleworkers are near accurate, Nigerian organizations must begin to understand how this work arrangement can be used to advance competitiveness.

BIBLIOGRAPHY

➢ Alexander, R. (2020), "Locked-Down Digital work". *International Journal of Information Management*. DOI: https://doi.org/10.1016/j.ijinfomgt.2020.102157

➢ Ahmadi, M., Helms. M., and Ross, T. (2000). "Technological developments: Shaping the teleworking environments of the future". *Facilities Journal, 18*(1/2), 83–89.

➢ Ajayi, P.I. (2020). "Telecommuting during Covid-19 in Nigeria". *African Journal for the Psychological study of Social Sciences*. 23(2).

➢ Allard, K., Haas, L. and Hwang, C.P. (2011). "Family-supportive Organizational Culture and Father's Experiences of Work-family Conflict in Sweden", *Gender, Work and Organization*, 18(2), pp. 141-157.

➢ Allen, Tammy D., Timothy D. Golden and Kristen M. Shockley. (2015), "How Effective is Telecommuting? Assessing the Status of our Scientific Findings". *Psychological Science in the Public Interest*.16(2), 40-68.

➢ Allert, J. (2001). "You're hired, now go home". *Training and Development, 55*(3), 54–58.

➢ Ansong, E. and Boateng, R (2017), "Organisational Adoption of Telecommuting: Evidence from a Developing Country". *Wiley online library.com*. DOI: https://doi.org/10.1002/isd2.12008

➢ Bailey, Diane E. and Nancy B. Kurland (2002), "A review of Telework Research: findings, new directions and lessons for the study of modern work". *Journal of Organizational Behaviour, 23*, 383-400.

➢ Baines, S. and Gelder, U. (2003). "What is Family friendly about the Workplace in the Home? The Case of Self-employed Parents and their Children", *New Technology, Work and Employment, 18*, pp. 223-234.

➢ Baruch, Y., and Nicholson, N. (1997). "Home, sweet work: Requirements for effective home working". *Journal of General Management, 23,* 15–30.

➢ Baruch, Y., and Yuen, Y. (2000). "Inclination to opt for teleworking: A comparative analysis of United Kingdom versus Hong Kong employees". *International Journal of Manpower, 21*(7), 531–539.

➢ Baumeister, R. and Leary, M. R. (1995). "The need to belong: Desire for interpersonal attachments as a fundamental human motivation". *Psychological Bulletin,* 117(3).

➢ Beastley, R.E., Lomo-David, E., and Seubert, V.R. (2001). "Telework and gender: Implications for the management of information technology professionals". *Industrial Management and Data Systems, 101*(9), 477–482.

➢ Belzunegui-Eraso, Al and Amaya, E (2020), "Teleworking in the Context of the COVID-19 Crisis". *Sustainability* 12, 3662. www.mdpi.com/journal/sustanability

➢ Benjamindada.com (2020). "How to be productive while working from home during COVID-19 pandemic", www.bejamindada.com/23-ways-to-be-productive-while-working-from-home

➢ Bick, R. *et al*. (2020). "A blueprint for remote working: Lessons from China". *McKinsey and Company*. 23 March.

➢ Buomprisco, G., Ricci, S., Perri, R. and De Sio, S. (2021). Health and Telework: New Challenges after COVID-19 Pandemic. *European Journal of Environment and Public Health*, 5(2), em0073. https://doi.org/10.21601/ejeph/9705

➢ Cartmill, C. (2020). "New survey shows 87% of staff wish to work from home in post lockdown world". *Belfast News Letter*. 28 May.

➢ Clark, S.C. (2000.) Work/ family Border Theory: A New Theory of Work/ family balance, *Human Relations*, 53(6), pp. 747-770, Google Scholar.

➤ Conner, D.S. (2003). "Social comparison in virtual work environments: An examination of contemporary referent selection". *Journal of Occupational and Organizational Psychology, 76*, 133–147.

➤ Curseu, P.L., Schalk, R., and Wessel, I. (2008). "How do virtual teams process information? A literature review and implications for management". *Journal of Managerial Psychology, 23*(6), 628–652.

➤ De Graaf, T. and Rietveld, P. (2007). "Substitution between working at home and out-of-home: The role of ICT and commuting costs". *Transportation Research Part A,* 41:142-160.

➤ Diefenbach, T. (2007). "The managerialistic ideology of organizational change management". *Journal of Organizational Change Management, 20*(1), 126–144.

➤ *Eurasia Review.* (2020). "Almost 90% Of Workers Would Be Willing To Continue Teleworking After The Pandemic". Eurasia Review. 4 May.

➤ Eurofound and the ILO. (2017). "Working anytime, anywhere: The effects on the world of work". Publications Office of the European Union, Luxembourg, and the International Labour Office, Geneva.

➤ Eurofound. (2020). "Living, working and COVID-19: First findings – April 2020". Dublin: Eurofound.

➤ Farrell, K. (2017). "Working from home: A double edged sword". *Home Renaissance Foundation Conference*, November 16-17, 2017, Royal Society of Medicine in London.

➤ Feldman, D. C., and Gainey, T. W. (1997). "Patterns of telecommuting and their consequences: Framing the research agenda". *Human Resource Management Review, 7,* 369–388.

➤ Felstead, A., Jewson, N. and Walters, S. (2005). *Changing Places of Work*, Palgrave Macmillan, Basingstoke.

➤ Ford, M., Heinen, B. and Langkamer, K. (2007). "Work and Family Satisfaction and Conflict: A Meta-analysis of Cross-domain Relations", *Journal of Applied Psychology*, 92(1), pp. 57-80.

➤ Fossilien, L and West Duff, M. (2020), "How to combat zoom fatigue". *Harvard Business Review.* https://hbr.org.2020/04/how-to-combat-zoom-fatigue

➤ Gajendran, R. S. and Harrison, D. A. (2006). *"The good, the bad, and the unknown about telecommuting: meta-analysis of individual consequences and mechanisms of distributed work*: Academy of Management Best Conference, held in USA".* Pennsylvania.

➤ Glenn Dutcher, E. (2012), "The Effects of Telecommuting on Productivity: An Experimental Examination. The Role of Dull and Creative Tasks". *Journal of Economic Behaviour and Organization, 84,* 355-363.

➤ Golden, T. D., Veiga, J. F. and Dino, R. N. (2008). "The impact of professional isolation on teleworker job performance and turnover intentions: Does time spent teleworking, interacting face-to-face, or having access to communication-enhancing technology matter?" *Journal of Applied Psychology*, 93(6):1412-1421.

➤ González, K., Fuentes, J. and Márquez, J. L. (2017). "Physical Inactivity, Sedentary Behavior and Chronic Diseases". *Korean journal of family medicine, 38*(3), 111-115. https://doi.org/10.4082/kjfm.2017.38.3.111

➤ Gorham, A. (2006). "Managing to Work: Why Mothers Need to Apply Workplace Skills in the Home", *Women in Management Review*, 3(4), pp 191-196.

➤ Grant, C.A., Wallace, L.M. and Spurgeon, P.C. (2013). "An Exploration of the Psychological Factors Affecting Remote e-worker's Job Effectiveness, Well-being and Work-life Balance", *Employee Relations*, 35(5), pp.527-546, https://doi.org/10.1108/ER-08-2012-0059

➤ Grant-Vallone, E.J. and Ensher, E.A. (2011). "An Examination of Work and Personal Life Conflict, Organizational Support, and Employee Health Among International Expatriates", *International Journal of Intercultural Relations*, 25(3), pp. 261-278.

➤ Hamilton, E.A., Gordon, J.R., and Whelan-Berry, K.S. (2006). "Understanding the work-life conflict of never-married women without children". *Women in Management Review, 21*(5), 393–415.

➤ Harbert, Anita and J. Tucker-Tatlow (2013), "Literature Review: Teleworking in Human services". *Southern Area Consortium of Human Services (SACHS)*, San Diego State University School of Social Work

➤ Harker, M.B. and MacDonnell, R. (2012). "Is Telework Effective for Organizations? A Meta- analysis of Empirical Research on Perceptions of Telework and Organizational Outcomes", *Management Research Review*, 35(7), pp. 602-616.

➤ Helms, M., and Raiszadeh, F. (2002). Virtual offices: Understanding and managing what you cannot see. *Work Study, 51*(4/5), 240–247.

➤ Helms, M.M. (1996), "Perspectives on Quality and Productivity for Competitive Advantage". *The TQM Magazine.* 8(3).

➤ Heneman, R.L., and Greenberger, D.B. (2002). *Human resource management in virtual organizations.* Columbus, Ohio: Ohio State University.

➤ Hoe, V., Urquhart, D., Kelsall, H. and Sim, M. (2012). "Ergonomic design and training for preventing work-related musculoskeletal disorders of the upper limb and neck in adults" (Review). *Cochrane Database of Systematic Reviewqs, 8*, Article No: CD008570. https://doi.org/10.1002/14651858.CD008570

➤ Horwitz, F.M., Bravington, D., and Silvis, U. (2006). "The promise of virtual teams: Identifying key factors in the effectiveness and failure". *Journal of European Industrial Training, 30*(6), 472–494.

➤ Huws, U., Gunnarsson, E., Weijers, T., Arvanitaki, K., and Trova, V. (1997), 'Teleworking: Guidelines for Good Practice". *Institute for Employment Studies* (iES), Report 329. University of Sussex, Brighton, United Kingdom.

➤ ILO. (2020a). *"Practical Guide on Teleworking during the COVID-19 pandemic and beyond. A practical guide".* Geneva: International Labour Office.

➤ ILO. (2020b). *"A policy framework for tackling the economic and social impact of the COVID-19 crisis".* ILO Policy Brief. Geneva: International Labour Office.

➤ ILO. (2020c). *"Work from home: Human factors/ergonomics considerations for teleworking".* Geneva: International Labour Office.

➤ ILO. (2020d). *"Managing work-related psychosocial risks during the COVID-19 pandemic".* Geneva: International Labour Office.

➤ ILO. (2020e). *"Keys for effective teleworking during the COVID-19 pandemic".* 26 March. Geneva: International Labour Office.

➤ Ilozor, D.B., and Ilozor, B.D. (2002). Australian teleworking: Management communication strategies. *Logistics Information Management, 15*(2), 80–87.

➤ Ingham, J. (2006). "Closing the talent management gap". *Strategic HR Review, 5*(3), 20–23.

➤ IoD. (2019), *"Managing Mental Health in Changing Business Models: Remote Working in SMEs. IoD Policy Report May 2019".* Institute of Directors, U.K.

➤ Jackson, P., Gharavi, H., and Klobas, J. (2006). "Technologies of the self: Virtual work and the inner panopticon". *Information Technology and People, 19*(3), 219–243.

➤ JALA International (2007), Jack Nilles. Retrieved from http://www.jala.com/jnmbio.php.

➤ Jensen, C., Finsen, L., Søgaard, K. and Christensen, H. (2002). "Musculoskeletal symptoms and duration of computer and mouse use". *International Journal Industrial Ergonomics, 30*(4-5), 265-275. https://doi.org/10.1016/S0169-8141(02)00130-0

➤ Johnson, J. (2004). "Flexible working: Changing the manager's role". *Management Decision, 42*(6), 721–737.

➤ Johnson, J. (2005). "The virtual workplace: The price is right". *Network World, 22*(36), 37.

➤ Joseph, S., Maurie J.C., Paul D. and Patrick S. (2020), "A Brave New World: Lessons from COVID-19 Pandemic for Transitioning to Sustainable Supply and Production". Resources Conservation and Recycling, DOI: https://doi.org/10.1016/j.resconrec.2020.104894

➤ Kepczyk, R. (1999). "Evaluating the virtual office". *Ohio CPA Journal, 58*(2), 16–17.

➤ Kossek, E.E., Lautsch, B.A. and Eaton, S.C. (2006). "Telecommuting, Control, and Boundary Management: Correlates of Policy Use and Practice, Job Control, and Work-family Effectiveness", *Journal of Vocational Behavior*, 68(2), pp. 347-367.

➤ Kowalski, K.B., and Swanson, J.A. (2005). "Critical success factors in developing teleworking programs". *Benchmarking: An International Journal, 12*(3), 236–249.

➤ Kreiner, G.E. (2006). "Consequences of Work-home Segmentation or Integration: A Person-environment Fit Perspective", *Journal of Organizational Behavior*, 27(4), pp. 485-507.

➤ Kreiner, G.E., Hollensbe, EC, Sheep, M.L. (2009). "Balancing Borders and Bridges: Negotiating the Work /home Interface Via Boundary Work Tactics", *Academy of Management Journal*, 52(4), pp. 704-730.

➤ Kurland, N. B. and Bailey, D. E. (1999). "Telework the advantages and challenges of working here, there, anywhere and anytime". *Organization Dynamics, 28*(2), 53-68. https://doi.org/10.1016/S0090-2616(00)80016-9

➤ Kurland, N., and Egan, T. (1999). "Teleworking: Justice and control in the virtual organization". *Organization Science, 10*(4), 500– 513.

➤ Lardi-Nadarajan, K. (2008). *Breathing a second life into the synthetic worlds*. New York: Deloitte MCS Limited.

➤ Lim, V.K.G., and Teo, T.S.H. (2000). "To work or not to work at home". *Journal of Managerial Psychology, 15*(6), 560–586.

➤ Madsen, S.R. (2011). "The Benefits, Challenges, and Implication of Teleworking: A Literature Review", *Journal of Culture and Religion*, 1(1), pp. 148-158.

➤ Mann, S. and Holdsworth, L. (2003). "The Psychological Impact of Teleworking: Stress, Emotions and Health", *New Technology, Work and Employment*, 18(3), pp. 196-211.

➤ Mann, S., Varey, R., and Button, W. (2000). "An exploration of the emotional impact of teleworking via computer-mediated communication". *Journal of Managerial Psychology, 15*(7), 668–690.

➤ Martinez-Sanchez, A., Perez-Perez, M., Vela-Jimenez, M.J., and De-Luis Carnicer, P. (2008). "Telework adoption, change management, and firm performance". *Journal of Organizational Change Management, 21*(1), 7–31.

➤ McKeever, V. (2020), "Coronavirus Lockdown are making the working day longer for many CNBC", www.cnbc.com

➤ Meadows, V. (2007). "Versatile bureaucracy: A telework case study". *The Public Manager, 36*(4), 33–37.

➤ Meyer, J.P., Srinivas, E.S., Lal, J.B., and Topolnytsky, L. (2007). "Employee commitment and support for an organizational change: Test of the three-component model in two cultures". *Journal of Occupational and Organizational Psychology, 180*, 185–211.

21

➢ Mirchandani, K. (2000). "The Best of Both Worlds' and 'Cutting My Own Throat': Contradictory Images of Home-based Work", *Qualitative Sociology,* 23(2), pp. 159-182.

➢ Morahan-Martin, J. and Schumacher, P. (2003). "Loneliness and social uses of the Internet". *Computer Human Behavior,* 19(6), 659-671. https://doi.org/10.1016/S0747-5632(03) 00040-2

➢ Morgan, R.E. (2004). "Teleworking: An Assessment of the Benefits and Challenges", *European Business Review,* 16(4), pp. 344-357.

➢ Moustafa-Leonard, K. (2007). "Trust and the manager-subordinate dyad: Virtual work as a unique context". *Journal of Behavioral and Applied Management, 8*(3), 197–201.

➢ Myjobmag, (2021). "Work from home challenges in Nigeria", www.myjobmag.com/blog/the-state-of-remote-work-in-nigeria

➢ Nätti, J., Anttila, T., Ojala, S. and Tammelin, M. (2009). *Paid Work at Home,* in Virolainen, H., Sirkemaa, S. and Vartiainen, T. (Eds), The Proceedings of the 14th International Conference on Telework, TUCS, Turku, Finland, pp. 173-185.

➢ Nätti, J., Tammelin, M., Anttila, T. and Ojala, S. (2011). "Work at Home and Time Use in Finland", *New Technology, Work and Employment,* 26(1), pp. 68-77.

➢ Neufeld, D.J and Fang, Y (2005), "Individual, Social and Situational determinants of Telecommuter Productivity". *Information and Management,* 42,1037-1049.

➢ Nytimescom. (2013). NY Times Sunday Review editorial: *Location, Location, Location,* available at www.nytimes.com/2013/03/03/

➢ O'Brien, T., and Hayden, H. (2007). Flexible work practices and the LIS sector: Balancing the needs of work and life? *Library Management, 29*(3), 199–228.

➢ Ojala, S, Natti, J, Anttila, T. (2014). Informal Overtime at Work instead of Telework: Increase in Negative Work-family Interface, *International Journal of Sociology and Social Policy,* 69-87.

➢ Pan, Cui and Qian (2020), "Information Resource and Orchestration during the COVID-19 Pandemic: A study of community lockdowns in China". *International Journal of Information Management.*

➢ Pathak, A.A., Bathini, D.R., Kandathil, G.M. (2015). "The Ban on Working from Home Makes Sense for Yahoo. It needs the Innovation and Speed of Delivery that come from Office-based Employees", *Human Resource Management International Digest,* 23(3), pp 12-14.

➢ Patrickson, M. (2002). Teleworking: "Potential employment opportunities for older workers?". *International Journal of Manpower, 23*(8), 704–715.

➢ Petersen, E., Wasserman S., Lee, S., Go, U., Holmes, A.H., Abri, S.A., Blumberg, L. and Tambyah, P. (2020), "COVID-19, we urgently need to start developing a exit strategy". *International Journal of Infectious Diseases.* DOI: 10.1016/j.ijrd.2020.04.035.

➢ Radcliff, J. (2010). "Working from Home: Issues and Strategies", 25 October 2010.

➢ Richard Ye, L. (2012). "Telecommuting: Implementation for Success". International Journal for Business and Social Science. 3(15).

➢ Richter, A., M.Leyer and M. Steinhuser (2020), "Workers United: Digitally enhancing social connectedness on the shop floor". *International Journal of Information Management.*

➢ Shareena, P. and Mahammad Shahid (2020), "Work from Home during COVID-19: Employees Perception and Experiences". *Global journal for Research Analysis* 9(5) DOI: 10.36106/gjra. May.

➢ Shekhar, S. (2006). Understanding the virtuality of virtual organisations. *Leadership and Organizational Development Journal, 27*(6), 465–483.

➢ Siha, S.M., and Monroe, R.W. (2006). "Teleworking's past and future: A literature review and research agenda". *Business Process Management Journal, 12*(4), 455–482

➢ Singh, Ravin, Myadam Akshay Kumar and Samuel T. Varghese (2017), "Impact of working Remotely on Productivity and Professionalism". *Journal of Business and Management.*, 19(5), 17-19.

➢ Smith, I. (2005). "Continuing professional development and workplace learning. Resistance to change – recognition and response". *Library Management, 26*(8/9), 519–522.

➢ Soenanto, Tuntas W., Djabir Hamzah, Mahlia Muis and Nurdim, Brasit (2016), "The Influence of Telecommuting Systems, Self-efficacy and the Quality of Management on work Productivity and the Competitiveness of Organizational Perspectives in Multinational Companies in Jakarta, Indonesia. *Scientific Research Journal*, vol. IV Issue III.

➢ Sorensen, H. (2016). "Best practices for managing telecommuting employees". Capella University. 30 September.

➢ Sperling, D., and Yeh, S. (2009). "Low carbon fuel standards". *Issues in Science and Technology, 25*(2), 57–66.

➢ Stanford, P. (2003). "Managing remote workers". *Executive Excellence, 20*(6), 6–7.

➢ Sullivan, C. (2003). What's in a Name? Definitions and Conceptualizations of Teleworking and Work at Home, *New Technology, Work and Employment*, 18(3), pp. 158-165.

➢ Sundaram, D.S., and Webster, C. (2000). "The role of nonverbal communication in service encounters". *Journal of Services Marketing, 14*(5), 378–391.

➢ Swink, D. R. (2008). "Telecommuter law: A new frontier in legal liability". *American Business Law,* 38(4):857-900.

➢ Thomée, S., Eklöf, M., Gustafsson, E., Nilsson, R. and Hagberg, M. (2007). "Prevalence of perceived stress, symptoms of depression and sleep disturbances in relation to information and communication technology (ICT) use among young adults. An explorative prospective study". *Computers in Human Behavior, 23*(3), 1300-1321. https://doi.org/10.1016/j.chb.2004.12.007

➢ Thorne, K. (2005). "Designing virtual organizations: Themes and trends in political and organisational discourses". *Journal of Management Development, 24*(7), 580–607.

➢ Tidd, R. (1999). "Establishing your virtual office". *Taxes, 77*(6), 6–7.

➢ Tietze, S. and Musson, G. (2010). Identity, Identity Work and the Experience of Working from Home, *Journal of Management Development, 29*(2), pp.148-156.

➢ Tietze, S., and Musson, G. (2003). The times and temporalities of home-based telework. *Personal Review, 32*(4), 438–455.

➢ Timbal, A. and Mustabsat, A. (2016). "Flexibility or Ethical Dilemma: An Overview of the Work from Home Policies in Modern Organizations around the World", *Human Resource Management International Digest, 24*(7)

➢ Wahlström, J. (2005). "Ergonomics, musculoskeletal disorders and computer work". *Occupational Medicine, 55*(3), 168-176. https://doi.org/10.1093/occmed/kqi083

➢ Watad, M.M., and Will, P.C. (2003). Telecommuting and organisational change: A middle-managers' perspective. *Business Process Management Journal, 9*(4), 459–472.

➤ Watson-Manheim, M.B., Chudoba, K.M., and Crowston, K. (2002). Discontinuities and continuities: A new way to understand virtual work. *Information Technology and People, 15*(3), 191–209.

➤ Wen, L. M., Kite, J. and Russel, C. (2010). "Is there a role for workplaces in reducing employees' driving to work? Findings from a cross-sectional survey from inner-west Sydney, Australia". *BMC Public Health,* 10(50):1-6.

➤ Wilsker, C. (2008). *Unleashing the hidden productivity of your small business.* New York: Avaya.

Lightning Source UK Ltd.
Milton Keynes UK
UKHW010759060223
416537UK00008B/1833